Rooted in Grace

POEMS of the REFORMED FAITH

Bruce W. Newcomer, Thd.

Big Bend Publishing

Copyright © 2025 by Bruce W. Newcomer

Paperback ISBN: 979-8-9993560-0-0

All rights reserved.

All rights reserved. This book or any portion thereof may not be reproduced or used in any manner whatsoever without the express written permission of the publisher except for the use of brief quotations in a book review.

"Scripture quotations are from the ESV® Bible (The Holy Bible, English Standard Version®), © 2001 by Crossway, a publishing ministry of Good News Publishers. ESV Text Edition: 2025. The ESV text may not be quoted in any publication made available to the public by a Creative Commons license. The ESV may not be translated in whole or in part into any other language. Used by permission. All rights reserved."

Layout and cover design by Bruce W. Newcomer

Contact at: bigbendpublishing@gmail.com

Contents

Introduction	1
1. By Faith Alone, Through Christ ALone	5
2. Freedom in the Spirit: A Poem on Romans 8:1-8	7
3. Life in the Spirit - Inspired by Romans 8:5-17	9
4. Inspired by 2 Timothy 3:16-17	17
5. Living in the Spirit	19
6. The Five Solas: A Poem	20
7. The Path of Grace	22
8. The Preacher's Voice	24
9. The Weight of Words	26
10. The Shepherd's Burden	28
11. In Shadows and in Sunlight	30
12. The Fire Within	32

13.	The Joy of Harvest	33
14.	A Prayer for Preachers	34
15.	The Eternal Echo	36
16.	The Shepherds Promise - Inspired by Psalm 23	38
17.	The Depths Within	40
18.	Chosen Before Time	42
19.	For Many, Not for All	44
20.	Irresistible Grace	47
21.	Eternal Security	50
22.	The Five Solas	53
23.	The Two Ways - Inspired by Psalm 1	59
24.	The Covenant Thread	65
25.	The Throne Above All Thrones	72
26.	The Heavens Declare - Inspired by Psalm 19	79
27.	Christ Crushes Satan - Inspired by Psalm 110	85
28.	The Gospel in the Garden - Inspired by Genesis 3 and the Belgic Confession Article 17	92
29.	The Pattern of All Prayer - Inspired by the Lord's Prayer	99
30.	The Ancient Declaration - Inspired by the Apostles' Creed	103
31.	The Tablets of Sinai: A Reformed Meditation	110
Conclusion		116

About the author

INTRODUCTION

The worn journal lay open on the desk, its pages yellowed with age and wisdom. Each line of verse carved into the paper spoke of struggles that stretched back to Eden, yet pointed forward to a hope that would never fade.

These poems emerge not from idle musings or romantic notions, but from the crucible of lived experience, where divine sovereignty meets human frailty. They wrestle with questions that had plagued believers throughout the centuries. How does one reconcile God's absolute control with the reality of suffering? Where does grace intersect with the grinding wheels of daily existence?

Reformed theology provides the scaffolding, but life supplies the flesh and blood. Calvin's careful expositions take on new meaning when filtered through midnight prayers in hospital waiting rooms. The Westminster Confession's precise language about predestination echoed differently after burying a child. Total depravity ceases being mere doctrine when confronting one's own capacity for betrayal.

Each poem in this collection traces a similar arc, beginning with human limitation, ascending to divine mystery, and landing somewhere between lament and doxology. They refuse simple answers. Instead, they embrace the tension that marked authentic faith: broken and whole, condemned and justified, dying and eternally alive.

The verses spoke to those who had tasted both wormwood and honey from the same providential hand. They address readers who understand that faith means more than positive thinking. It means clinging to promises when circumstances scream their denial. These are poems for people who have learned that sovereignty provides not exemption from trials but presence within them.

Some stanzas explore the doctrine of election through the lens of ordinary moments: a mother watching her sleeping infant, a farmer surveying drought-stricken fields, an elderly saint facing their final sunset. Others grapple with sanctification's slow work, comparing it to erosion carving canyons or seeds germinating in darkness. The imagery stays earthy, tactile, refusing to float into abstraction.

This collection avoids both extremes that often plagued religious poetry. It neither dissolved into shapeless mysticism nor calcified into rigid dogma. Instead, it maintains the Reformed tradition's commitment to engaging both heart and mind. Theological precision danced with emotional honesty. Scriptural allusions weave through contemporary observations without feeling forced or decorative.

Readers will find echoes of the Psalms' raw honesty, Job's unflinching questions, and Paul's soaring doxologies. But they would also encounter grocery store epiphanies, highway revelations, and kitchen table conversations with doubt. The sacred and mundane intermingled because Reformed theology insists that all of life falls under God's sovereign care.

The poems refuse to smooth over difficulties. They acknowledge the scandal of particularity, that God chose some and not others. They wrestle with the problem of evil without retreating into philosophical abstractions. They confront the cost of discipleship without minimizing its weight. Yet through it all runs a golden thread of grace, unearned and unstoppable.

Some verses take familiar biblical narratives and illuminate them from unexpected angles. Abraham's near-sacrifice of Isaac became a meditation on trusting promises that seemed to contradict themselves. Jacob's midnight wrestling match transforms into every believer's struggle with divine mystery. The prodigal son's return speaks to anyone who has ever doubted their welcome in the Father's house.

The language throughout remains accessible without being simplistic. Complex theological concepts translated into images anyone can grasp: sanctification as bread rising, justification as adoption papers signed in blood, glorification as dawn, breaking after endless night. These poems trust the reader's intelligence while honoring their need for beauty.

This collection arrives at a cultural moment desperate for depth. In an age of tweets and sound bites, these verses demand slower reading, deeper reflection. They resist the therapeutic deism that reduces God to a cosmic life coach. Instead, they present a sovereign Lord who works through suffering rather than around it, who ordains both tears and laughter for purposes beyond human comprehension.

The poems will comfort the afflicted and afflict the comfortable. They offer no cheap grace, no easy believism. But for those willing to wrestle, to doubt, to cling despite everything, they provide companionship on the narrow road. They remind readers that others had walked this path, Augustine and Luther, Edwards and Spurgeon, countless unnamed saints who chose faith over sight.

Each page testifies to the Reformed conviction that all truth is God's truth, whether discovered in Scripture, nature, or human experience. The poems draw from literature, history, science, and art, recognizing that common grace scattered beauty throughout creation. Yet they maintain the distinction between general and special revelation, between admiring creation and worshiping the Creator.

By Faith Alone, Through Christ Alone

Upon the edge of striving years,
  Where shadows crowd a heavy mind,
  The heart, awash in doubts and fears,
  Seeks peace it cannot seem to find.
  Not by the toil of weary hands,
  Nor by the sum of good deeds done,
  Not by the laws or man's commands—
  But by the gift of God the Son.
  O precious grace! Unmerited,
  A wellspring flowing, pure and free,
  For all the debts I owed are paid
  Upon the Cross at Calvary.
  No silver coin, no offering,
  No ladder stretched from earth to sky,

Could grant the soul redeeming wings
Or bid the spirit learn to fly.
But faith—so simple, true, and small—
Believes the promise, dares to rest
In Christ, who gave His life for all,
The lost, the weary, and oppressed.
By faith alone, through Christ alone,
The doors of mercy open wide;
No other hope, no other throne—
He stands, my Advocate, my Guide.
So let my boast be this alone:
The love that found and carried me,
For through His blood, and not my own,
I stand forgiven, wholly free.

Freedom in the Spirit: A Poem on Romans 8:1-8

There is now no condemnation -
   A morning dawns, serene and bright -
   For those in Christ, a new creation,
   Transformed by faith, restored to light.
   The law once chained the soul in longing,
   With flesh and weakness pulling down;
   Yet Love descended, gently drawing
   Hearts from shadow, thorns, and frown.
   What law could not, the Spirit renders -
   Life breathes in, as death retreats;
   No longer slaves to guilt's defenders,
   The heart with hope and mercy beats.
   Set free from sin, our minds awaken
   To Spirit's wind, to holy peace;

The flesh's voice grows faint, forsaken,
While grace and truth in us increase.
To set one's mind on fleeting pleasures
Brings restless moments, empty days;
But life and peace are Spirit's treasures,
A golden path, a sunlit gaze.
So walk no more in fear's dominion,
Let every chain at last be loosed;
For in Christ's love and Spirit's union,
We rise, forgiven, and renewed.

LIFE IN THE SPIRIT - INSPIRED BY ROMANS 8:5-17

THE MIND SET ON the flesh meant death,
    A rotting corpse with moving breath.
    Each thought corrupt, each motive stained,
    Each desire by sin constrained.
    The carnal mind at war with God,
    Could not submit beneath His rod.
    Hostile to His holy ways,
    Darkened through its numbered days.
    But those who walked by Spirit's power
    Found life and peace in every hour.
    Not by their strength or righteous deeds,
    The Spirit sowed these holy seeds.
    Reformed truth held this treasure tight:
    That God alone could grant new sight.

No human will could break sin's chain,
The Spirit must make all things plain.
For who among the sons of earth
Could give themselves a second birth?
Who could change their nature's core
From death to life forevermore?
The flesh sold under sin's dark reign
Could never make itself unstained.
Like leopards trying to change their spots,
Or corpses rising from their plots.
But God, rich in His mercy deep,
Awakened those who lay asleep.
The Spirit moved on hearts of stone,
Made rebels bow before the throne.
Not because they chose Him first,
He satisfied their deepest thirst.
Monergistic grace broke through,
What human effort couldn't do.
Those led by God's own Spirit bright
Were sons of God, brought to the light.
Not slaves who cringed beneath the lash,
Not hirelings working just for cash.
But children crying "Abba" loud,
Adopted into glory's crowd.
The Spirit testified within
That they were His, redeemed from sin.
This wasn't mere religious talk
Or rules about the way to walk.
The Spirit dwelt within their frame,

ROOTED IN GRACE

Set their cold hearts all aflame.
The same power that raised Christ Jesus
From death's grip that tried to seize us
Now worked in every blood-bought soul,
Making broken sinners whole.
Paul painted pictures stark and clear,
You're either there or you are here.
No middle ground, no neutral space,
You're either dead or saved by grace.
The mind of flesh could never please
The God who spoke the galaxies.
Its best attempts were filthy rags,
Its righteousness just boastful brags.
But transformation came complete
When Spirit made the work replete.
Not reformation of the old,
But resurrection, bright as gold.
New creatures with new appetites,
New loves, new joys, and new delights.
The things they hated, now they loved,
The things they loved, by grace removed.
Consider how the Scripture spoke
To those whom Spirit's power woke:
"If Christ is in you," Paul declared,
"Though death your body hasn't spared
Because of sin's remaining stain,
Your spirit lives, no more sin's chain."
The body groaned beneath the curse,
But inward man grew none the worse.

And more, that mortal flesh would rise
When Christ descended from the skies.
The Spirit dwelling deep within
Guaranteed victory over sin.
Not just the soul made pure and bright,
But bodies raised in glory's light.
Creation's groan would find its end
When Christ returned, our Friend.
The obligation shifted ground,
No longer to the flesh were bound
Those whom the Spirit made alive,
No longer did they merely strive
To keep the law by human power,
But Spirit-led in every hour.
The law written on hearts of flesh,
Not stone tablets, cold and fresh.
To live according to the flesh
Led to a death both sure and fresh.
But putting deeds of body dead
By Spirit's power, life instead.
Not asceticism's harsh regime,
Nor mystic's esoteric dream,
But daily dying to sin's call
Through Him who conquered once for all.
The Spirit of adoption cried
Within the hearts of those who died
To self and sin and Satan's claim,
Who bore reproach for Jesus' name.
Not cowering in servile fear,

But knowing God as Father dear.
The same word Jesus used in prayer
Now on their lips, beyond compare.
"Abba, Father!" Hearts set free
Could cry with bold intensity.
Not formal, distant deity,
But Dad who bounced them on His knee.
The Spirit witnessed with their spirit,
This truth they could always inherit:
They were children of the King,
Heirs of everything.
Joint-heirs with Christ! The mind could reel
At what this covenant made real.
Everything the Son possessed
Became theirs too, forever blessed.
His righteousness, their covering wore,
His inheritance, their store.
His Father, now their Father too,
His destiny, their avenue.
But suffering marked the path to glory,
Every saint could tell that story.
If they suffered with their Lord,
Glory followed, heaven's reward.
Not suffering that they had earned
For foolishness, but what concerned
Their witness to a hostile world
Where Satan's banners were unfurled.
Reformed believers understood
This suffering was for their good.

God's providence arranged each trial,
Refining gold from what was vile.
No random chance or cosmic dice,
But Father's wisdom, precise.
Each tear counted, each groan heard,
Each promise in His holy Word.
The Spirit helped them in their weakness,
When prayers seemed to die in bleakness.
With groans too deep for human speech,
The Spirit prayed what they couldn't reach.
Perfect intercession made
For saints who felt so deeply frayed.
The Comforter lived up to name,
Set trembling hearts once more aflame.
Life in the Spirit meant new eyes
To see through earth's deceptive lies.
Where others saw just random pain,
They saw their Father's loving reign.
Where others felt abandoned, alone,
They knew they'd never be disowned.
The Spirit sealed them for that day
When Christ would come to lead the way.
No condemnation! Trumpet sound
For those in Christ Jesus found!
The law of sin and death dethroned,
The law of life in Spirit owned.
What law could never do, held fast
By flesh too weak, was done at last
When God sent forth His only Son,

The victory forever won.
Those walking not by flesh's lead
But as the Spirit gave them speed
Found righteousness the law required
Was theirs, by grace acquired.
Not their own works, but Christ's alone,
Imputed, made their very own.
The Spirit worked this faith within,
The gift of God, not born of sin.
Life in the Spirit bloomed and grew,
Made all things bright and all things new.
Not perfection, sin remained,
But sin no longer fully reigned.
The struggle real, the battle fierce,
But victory would evil pierce.
For He who raised Christ from the grave
Had power still to seek and save.
Reformed theology held this chain:
Election's choice before time's reign,
Effectual calling breaking through,
Regeneration, life made new,
Justification, peace with God,
Adoption in the family's pod,
And sanctification's daily fight,
Till glorification's endless light.
The Spirit worked through every stage,
From first to last, through every age.
Not human will that ebbed and flowed,
But sovereign grace that overrode.

Irresistible, yet somehow sweet,
Making rebels kiss His feet.
Not forced against their deepest will,
But will transformed by sovereign skill.
Life in the Spirit, gift supreme,
Beyond earth's highest, wildest dream.

Inspired by 2 Timothy 3:16-17

All Scripture's breath, a holy wind,
   That stirs the soul, renews within -
   From ancient scroll and whispered line,
   A lamp that leads through every time.
   God-breathed and living, shaped to teach,
   It shows the heart what truth can reach,
   Reveals the flaws, corrects the mind,
   Restores the wayward, makes us kind.
   For doctrine, reproof, each gentle art,
   Instruction meant to shape the heart,
   That all who seek and all who yearn
   May from its wisdom richly learn.
   Equipped for every work of grace,
   Prepared to run the faithful race,
   The sacred Word, both sword and seed,

Supplies the strength for every need.
So let us hold this gift so true,
Its purpose vast, its vision new -
For every life it will refine,
And show the world a love divine.

Living in the Spirit

Not of the flesh, but of the Spirit's embrace,
   A dwelling eternal, a sanctified space.
   If the Spirit of God resides within,
   Then life begins, freedom from sin.
   The flesh may falter, its days are but few,
   Yet the Spirit breathes life, pure and true.
   A power so vast, it raised Christ from the grave,
   A promise of hope, a soul to save.
   Through Him who dwells, the mortal transforms,
   Awakened anew, where His light warms.
   Death defeated, its shadow erased,
   Eternal life, by the Spirit's grace.
   So live in the Spirit, let the flesh fade,
   For in His presence, no fear is displayed.
   Romans 8 whispers, to all who will hear,
   Life in the Spirit, ever so near.

The Five Solas: A Poem

In ancient halls where echoes rise,
   A song endures, unwavering, bright—
   Five banners, woven by sacred ties,
   Bear hope through the longest night.
   Scripture Alone - the lamp aflame,
   Whose ancient pages, bold and sure,
   Reveal the heart, the holy Name,
   The truth unchanging, rich and pure.
   Christ Alone - Redeemer, King,
   The only bridge from earth to throne;
   Upon His mercy do we cling,
   His love and life is our cornerstone.
   Faith Alone - no purchase made,
   No deed can tip the holy scale;
   By trusting hearts, not works displayed,

ROOTED IN GRACE

We find the path, though we may fail.
Grace Alone - a gift so vast,
Unmerited, it freely flows;
The chains of sin are loosed at last,
As morning in the soul arose.
To God Alone Be Glory - sing!
Let boast and pride in shadow fall;
The heavens and the angels ring,
For God is all in all.
O, fivefold light that guides our way,
Enduring through the storms we face—
Upon these truths our souls shall stay,
Upheld forever by His grace.

THE PATH OF GRACE

Upon a quiet hillside, where olive branches sway,
A gentle voice once whispered truths the world could not gainsay.
He spoke of love unending, of mercy's boundless sea,
And beckoned every weary soul, "Come, follow, trust in Me."
No ladder built of human hands ascends to heaven's light,
No ancient law or noble deed can heal the soul's blight.
Yet in the garden, dew-drenched, beneath the starry dome,
He bore the weight of sorrow's curse - so every heart finds home.
Through thorn-strewn path and crimson cross, His sacrifice was made,
A gate flung wide for all who seek the shelter of His shade.

No other name, no other way, the scriptures gently claim,

But Christ, the Lamb, the Living Way, salvation's holy flame.

O wanderer upon the road, with burdens hard to bear,

Lift up your eyes, for grace abounds - He meets you in your prayer.

In trust and faith, surrender all, let every doubt be stilled:

For Jesus walked the way alone, that all might be fulfilled.

So let us journey, hand in hand, along this path of love,

Our hearts made whole, our hope restored, by Him who reigns above.

For in His name salvation lives, the truth, the life, the way -

And those who call upon the Lord shall never go astray.

THE PREACHER'S VOICE

Upon a dawn both grave and bright,
  I rise and don the preacher's coat -
  Not of silk or velvet white,
  But humble cloth and hope remote.
  I walk the road, both dust and dew,
  Where countless feet have journeyed through,
  With trembling heart and steady mind,
  Entrusted with the words divine.
  Before the pulpit's ancient wood,
  Or in the fields where lilies grow,
  I stand as witness, as I should,
  To seeds of truth I long to sow.
  The lamp is lit, the oil is poured,
  The Book is open, Spirit stored -
  A preacher not by pride or fame,

But called to speak the sacred Name.

THE WEIGHT OF WORDS

To preach is not for self to speak,
   Nor simply voice the things I know -
   But channel words the weary seek,
   And let God's living waters flow.
   The scroll unrolls, its stories old,
   From Sinai's fire to Bethlehem,
   From prophets bold, and shepherds told,
   To Calvary's sacrificial lamb.
   The Word is not a story passed,
   But breath and light, a burning coal;
   It wrestles with the heart downcast,
   And gently carves the jagged soul.
   My lips must muster courage true,
   To share of mercy always new -
   Not for persuasion's fleeting prize,

But that the soul in darkness rise.

The Shepherd's Burden

I walk among both lost and found,
  With gentle hand and listening ear;
  Some hearts are thorns, some fertile ground,
  Some closed in grief, some drawn by fear.
  Each Sunday's bell, each weekday's call,
  I bear the burdens, great and small,
  Of saints who gather, fold, and stray,
  And those who falter on the way.
  For preaching is a shepherd's art -
  To call the scattered, bind the torn,
  To comfort those with shattered heart,
  To cradle broken dreams forlorn.
  The sermon is not simply speech,
  But balm and bridge, a hand outstretched;
  For every word I dare to teach

Is born of prayers both fierce and wretched.

In Shadows and in Sunlight

The preacher walks where shadows fall,
   With questions deep as ancient wells;
   There are no easy answers, all
   The soul's great mysteries no voice dispels.
   Yet in the silence, Spirit's sigh,
   I find the courage to reply -
   Not with the wisdom of the wise,
   But with the faith that still defies.
   Some days the pews are nearly bare,
   The world's distractions drawing hearts;
   Yet still I offer up my prayer,
   And trust the Spirit does its part.
   For one who hears, one heart made whole,
   One soul imperfect, yet made bold -
   The task is worth each doubt and pain,

Each tearful night and hopeful strain.

THE FIRE WITHIN

WOE TO ME IF I do not speak
  The ancient prophet's cry rings true;
  A fire burns I cannot keep,
  A love that must break forth anew.
  It is not mine to guard or hoard,
  But share the riches of the Lord,
  To comfort, challenge, teach, and bless,
  And testify through wilderness.
  The hands I lift in blessing's form
  Are scarred by labor, fear, and loss;
  But still I rise, though torn and worn,
  To point the weary to the cross.
  The world may laugh, may turn away,
  Yet still the call will bid me stay -
  For peace and hope in God's domain
  Are worth the cost, are worth the pain.

The Joy of Harvest

To see a child in wonder gaze
   At stories old, yet ever new -
   To watch the elder lift their praise,
   And hear, "I see God's love in you" -
   These are the treasures none can steal,
   The silent joys that preachers feel;
   For every heart that finds its song
   Makes all the striving well and strong.
   Baptisms in rivers clear,
   Weddings under vaulted skies,
   Confessions whispered, drawing near,
   And final blessings as one dies -
   A preacher stands at every gate,
   Both birth and death and all between,
   Entrusted with the threads of fate,
   A witness to the things unseen.

A Prayer for Preachers

God, give me words both true and kind,
   And courage when the night is long;
   Let not my mouth or doubting mind
   Betray the hope within Your song.
   Let every lesson, every prayer,
   Be offered up with humble care -
   Not for my glory, but for You,
   That lives be changed and hearts made new.
   May I be servant, not a king;
   A lamp, not sun, to light the way.
   May I rejoice in everything
   That brings Your word to life today.
   May those who hear not see my face,
   But glimpse instead Your amazing grace—
   And as I preach, may I be led

By You, whose love is daily bread.

THE ETERNAL ECHO

Preaching is not a fleeting task,
   But echoes down through rolling years;
   It is a flame in earthen flask,
   A song that lingers past our tears.
   For long after my voice is still,
   And all my words have slipped away,
   The seeds I scatter, if God will,
   May spring to life in someone's day.
   So let me preach with all my breath,
   With every fiber, every part;
   Let love be stronger still than death,
   And faith the anchor of my heart.
   For preaching is a gift, a trust -
   To point beyond what eyes can see,
   To speak of hope, to lift the dust,
   To share the light that sets us free.
   Let every word be sown in love.

Let every sermon serve as seed.
Let God be glorified above,
And hearts find all the grace they need.
Amen.

The Shepherds Promise - Inspired by Psalm 23

IN MEADOWS LUSH WHERE shadows flee,
The Lord, my shepherd, watches me.
His staff and rod provide their rest,
Beside still waters, I am blessed.
When pathways dark obscure my sight,
His presence turns the dark to light.
Through valleys deep where death looms near,
His comfort banishes my fear.
A table spread before my foes,
My cup with mercy overflows.
My head anointed with His oil,
My soul finds rest from earthly toil.
His goodness follows where I roam,
His kindness leads me safely home.

In His sweet dwelling I shall be,
Restored by grace eternally.
The Shepherd knows each lamb by name,
His faithful love remains the same.
Though mountains move and oceans roar,
I'll dwell with Him forevermore.

The Depths Within

There exists no righteous soul,
   Not one that stands unmarred,
   No heart that comprehends the whole,
   No seeker after God.
   Our minds in hostile rebellion bent,
   Against divine decree.
   Our wills by nature cannot consent
   To laws we cannot see.
   The flesh, a prison of our pride,
   Cannot please God above.
   Our very nature testifies
   We spurn His perfect love.
   No corner of our hearts untouched
   By sin's pervasive stain.
   We grasp for glory, clutch and clutch,
   Yet only harvest pain.
   Apart from grace we cannot turn,

Our steps lead far astray.
The truth we desperately should learn:
We cannot find the Way.
Total our fall from Eden's light,
Complete our inner night,
Until His mercy makes things right
And grants us second sight.
For in our depravity complete,
His grace shines all the more,
When mercy and our justice meet
At Christ's redeeming door.

Chosen Before Time

Not by human will or strength,
   Nor by wisdom, wealth, or worth,
   Before the stars were set in place,
   Before the mountains found their birth.
   "No one comes unless I draw,"
   The Savior's words ring clear and true.
   Not our seeking found His grace,
   But His seeking first found you.
   In love He marked us as His own,
   Before creation's dawn had stirred,
   Inscribed our names within His book,
   Our destiny secured by Word.
   Who can fathom depths so vast?
   This mystery of sovereign choice,
   That God would know us, name us, claim us,
   Before we had a voice.
   Foreknown, forenamed, foreloved by God,

According to His perfect plan,
Not based on future faith foreseen,
But purposed ere the world began.
Predestined to be like His Son,
Conformed to Christ's own sacred face,
First chosen, then in time called forth,
Recipients of stunning grace.
No pride can stand before this truth,
No merit did our souls display.
When dead in sin, blind to His light,
He chose us anyway.
This is no cold, capricious act,
But love's most perfect, precious gift.
The Father draws us to the Son,
Our fallen souls to lift.
What comfort in this doctrine deep,
What peace amid life's raging sea,
That God's election stands secure,
Anchored in eternity.

For Many, Not for All

THE NARROW GATE STANDS open wide,
   Yet few there be who enter in.
   While broad the road to death and hell,
   Where multitudes march bound in sin.
   "This cup," He said, "my blood outpoured,
   For many for remission given."
   Not waste, but purpose marked His death,
   A perfect plan designed in heaven.
   In Antioch the Gentiles heard,
   The word of life, the gospel true.
   And who believed? The text is clear:
   Those God ordained, no less, no new.
   His death, sufficient for all men,
   Efficient for His chosen sheep.
   The Shepherd knows for whom He died,

His covenant of love to keep.
No drop of sacred blood was spilled
Without intent, without design.
Each crimson stain had purpose true,
Each pain inflicted was divine.
For every soul the Father gave,
The Son would purchase with His life.
Not one would perish, not one lost,
Through all the world's tumultuous strife.
Not universal was His aim,
When hanging on that cursed tree.
But particular His saving grace,
For those the Father gave to be.
The mystery of grace divine,
That Christ would die for certain men.
Not for the mass of human race,
But for His church, His brethren.
Does this diminish saving work?
Or limit God's majestic plan?
Nay, it exalts His sovereign will,
And humbles prideful heart of man.
For who are we to question Him,
The Potter with His yielding clay?
To shape some vessels for His use,
While others stored for judgment day.
His atonement, limited by love,
Designed with perfect wisdom's skill.
That none for whom Christ bled and died
Would ever face eternal ill.

The narrow gate, the precious blood,
The souls ordained since time began.
Three witnesses to one great truth:
Salvation is God's sovereign plan.
No universal pardon bought,
No wasted grace upon the cross.
But perfect purchase, full atonement,
Ensuring none of His be lost.
So marvel at this truth profound,
That Christ died not for all mankind,
But for His bride, His chosen ones,
Those in the Book of Life enshrined.
The Savior's blood, of infinite worth,
Could save ten thousand worlds or more.
Yet purposed for His elect alone,
Those whom the Father set in store.
What comfort in this doctrine deep,
What rest for weary souls to know,
That Christ's atonement, fixed in scope,
Ensures His sheep to heaven go.
No chance or change can thwart His will,
No soul He purchased slip away.
Limited in scope, unlimited in power,
This truth lights our darkest day.

Irresistible Grace

When He calls, the dead must rise,
   No soul can spurn His loving voice.
   The clay reshaped by Potter's hands,
   Has never had another choice.
   "All that the Father gives to me
   Will come," the Savior's promise rings.
   Not might, or could, or may perhaps,
   But will, as certain as He brings.
   The Spirit's work, like wind unseen,
   Blows where it wishes, none resists.
   No human will can thwart this call,
   When God upon His child insists.
   Called, justified, and glorified,
   The golden chain unbroken stands.
   No link will fail, no soul escape,
   When clasped within the Father's hands.
   We did not choose Him, truth be told,

Dead spirits cannot seek the light.
But grace, invincible and sure,
Restored our hearts, gave blinded sight.
Lazarus bound in grave clothes tight,
Did not decide to leave the tomb.
The Master's voice that spoke with power,
Compelled him from death's darkened room.
So too our souls enslaved to sin,
Could not desire the things above.
Until that moment swift and sure,
When grace descended, wrapped in love.
Effectual calling, sovereign work,
Not gentle nudge or mild request.
But resurrection power displayed,
As hearts of stone faced heaven's test.
No sinner saved against his will,
Yet none whose will remained unchanged.
The Spirit's art: to make us willing,
Our deepest longings rearranged.
What glory in this truth profound,
That none can thwart God's saving plan.
When He determines to redeem,
No force in hell or earth or man.
Those He predestined, these He called,
And those He called, He justified.
The work begun will be completed,
In Christ the end is ratified.
From death to life, from dark to light,
From bondage into freedom sweet.

Grace irresistible, divine,
Makes salvation wholly complete.
No credit can we claim or take,
No room for boasting in this tale.
For even faith itself was granted,
When grace refused to let us fail.
The Father draws, the Spirit seals,
The Son receives all given Him.
A perfect work, a perfect plan,
That reaches to our soul's dark rim.
So rest, dear saint, in this sweet truth:
Your coming to the cross was sure.
Not by your strength or wisdom gained,
But by His grace, divine and pure.
The call that brought you to your knees,
Was backed by all of heaven's might.
Irresistible in gentle power,
It turned your darkness into light.
For whom He calls, He also keeps,
No sheep can wander from His fold.
The work begun will be completed,
As ancient prophets long foretold.
All hail the power of sovereign grace,
That conquers every rebel heart.
When He determines to redeem,
No soul can stand His love apart.

Eternal Security

"I GIVE THEM ETERNAL life, and they shall never perish;
   no one will snatch them out from my hand."
   Once grasped by grace, forever held,
   No power can break that sacred bond.
   The Shepherd keeps His treasured sheep,
   No wolf can drag them to despond.
   "Whoever hears my word," He said,
   "And trusts in Him who sent me here,
   Has crossed from death to life indeed."
   What blessed promise, strong and clear!
   No condemnation now remains
   For those found safe in Christ the Lord.
   The debt was paid on Calvary's hill,
   When wrath and mercy strangely warred.
   The Father's hand, the Son's firm grip,
   A double clasp no force can break.
   What God has joined, what Christ has sealed,

ROOTED IN GRACE

No power in hell can ever take.
We did not earn this firm embrace,
Nor can we lose what was not gained
By human merit, works, or worth,
Our standing is by blood obtained.
The Spirit's seal, a guarantee,
A down payment of glory's day.
The One who started this good work
Will finish what He began, His way.
Some doubt may cloud the pilgrim's path,
When sin entangles weary feet.
But deeper than our fickle hearts,
God's faithfulness stands firm, complete.
Like Israel led through desert lands,
Through wandering ways and faithless fears,
God's covenant love remained unchanged
Throughout those long and painful years.
True saints persevere not by might,
Not by their strength or willful choice.
They press ahead because they're kept,
Because they've heard the Shepherd's voice.
The branch that's truly grafted in
Cannot be severed from the vine.
The life that flows from Christ Himself
Ensures the weakest branch will thrive.
What blessed rest this truth affords!
What peace amid life's raging sea!
That neither death nor life nor powers
Can separate Christ's love from me.

Not that we cannot fall or stray,
The path holds many a stumbling stone.
But He who chose us from the first
Will never leave His own alone.
The warnings in the sacred text
Serve as the means God's grace employs.
They frighten sheep from dangerous cliffs,
As loving parents use stern voice.
So press ahead with holy fear,
Yet confidence in Christ alone.
The Author and Finisher of faith
Will guide you safely, bring you home.
When Satan whispers dark with doubt,
When conscience screams of failures past,
Look not within but up to Him
Whose righteousness is yours, steadfast.
Once justified, forever just,
God's verdict stands through endless days.
His children stumble, yes, but rise,
Upheld by everlasting grace.
No name erased from heaven's book,
No living stone torn from the wall,
No sheep snatched from the Shepherd's care,
His promise stands: He keeps them all.

THE FIVE SOLAS

SCRIPTURE ALONE, THE BEDROCK stands,
  Not councils, creeds, or human hands.
  The Word of God, both sharp and sweet,
  Makes wisdom's path beneath our feet.
  No pope presides, no tradition binds
  Beyond what sacred scripture finds.
  The prophets spoke, apostles penned,
  And there, God's revelation ends.
  By Scripture's light we test all things,
  Each doctrine that the preacher brings.
  Like Bereans of noble mind,
  We search to see what truths we find.
  The Book speaks clear to humble hearts,
  Though scholars parse its every part.
  The plowboy reading by his fire
  Can grasp what learned men require.
  Not that we cast off wisdom past,

The saints before us labored fast.
But even Augustine must bow
When Scripture speaks its verdict now.
The creeds we love, the councils prize,
Stand only as they harmonize
With what the prophets long foretold
And apostolic pens made bold.
Grace alone, the sovereign gift,
No merit helps the soul to lift.
From first to last, from start to end,
On grace alone we must depend.
Not grace that meets us halfway there,
Not grace that human will must share.
But grace that raises dead men up,
Grace that fills an empty cup.
Before we sought, He came to find.
Before we woke, He healed the blind.
Before we reached, He grasped us tight.
Before we loved, He brought us light.
The drowning man contributes naught
Except the sin that judgment brought.
The Lifeguard plunges, bears the cost,
And hauls to shore the one thought lost.
Amazing grace, how sweet the sound!
That saved a wretch like me, once bound.
I once was lost but now am found,
Was blind but now can see around.
Faith alone, the empty hand
That grasps what grace has fully planned.

Not faith plus works, not faith plus rite,
Just trusting Christ makes sinners right.
The jailer asked with trembling voice,
"What must I do?" One simple choice,
"Believe upon the Lord," Paul said,
"And you'll be saved from sin and dread."
No pilgrimage to distant shrine,
No penance harsh or discipline.
No ladder climbed by human strength,
No righteous deeds of any length.
Faith looks away from self to Christ,
Where mercy flows from sacrifice.
Faith rests upon another's work,
Not striving in the moral murk.
The thief upon the cross had naught,
No baptism, no good deeds wrought.
Just faith that looked to Christ and cried,
"Remember me!" And Jesus replied.
Like Abraham, who trusted God,
And righteousness was his reward.
Not for the works his hands had done,
But faith in God's promised Son.
The hand of faith itself is weak,
But mighty is the One we seek.
Faith's power lies not in its grip,
But in the Rock on which we're fixed.
Christ alone, the cornerstone,
No other name beneath heaven's throne.
Not Christ and Mary, Christ and saints,

Not Christ plus human restraints.
One mediator stands between
The Holy God and sinners unclean.
The God-man bridges heaven's span,
Fully divine, yet fully man.
No saint in glory intercedes,
No priest on earth for sinners pleads,
Save Christ who sits at God's right hand,
Our Advocate who understands.
He is the Way, no other road
Leads to the Father's blessed abode.
He is the Truth, all else is lie
That promises to sanctify.
He is the Life, apart from Him
We wither like a severed limb.
In Christ alone our hope is found,
He is our light, our strength, our song.
This cornerstone, this solid ground,
Firm through the fiercest drought and storm.
As long as Christ the Lord is found,
Our anchor holds within the veil.
Not Buddha's path of enlightenment,
Not Mohammad's laws of government,
Not Hindu gods in countless forms,
Christ only saves, Christ only warms.
When conscience speaks its guilty verdict,
When Satan brings his accusations,
We plead not personal perfection,
But Christ's complete justification.

ROOTED IN GRACE

Glory to God alone we raise,
The Alpha and Omega praise.
Not glory shared with human pride,
But all to Him who lived and died.
From Him all blessings freely flow,
Through Him all wisdom we can know,
To Him all honor must return,
For Him alone our hearts should burn.
The preacher in his pulpit high
Must point away from human eye.
Not eloquence or learning's show,
But Christ, and Him crucified below.
The saint who serves in hidden ways,
The martyr earning world's dark praise,
The missionary crossing seas,
All work for God's glory, not to please.
When good works flow from blood-bought hands,
When love obeys what God commands,
The glory goes not to the stream,
But to the Fountain, the Supreme.
In heaven's courts, no boasting rings
Of human works or offerings.
Ten thousand times ten thousand cry,
"Worthy the Lamb alone on high!"
These five alone, solas styled,
Stand against what man has piled.
Reforms that swept through Europe's land
Still guide the faithful's pilgrim band.
Scripture alone to light our way,

Grace alone to save the stray,
Faith alone to grasp the gift,
Christ alone our souls to lift,
Glory to God alone we give,
On these five truths we die and live.
When Rome had added layer thick
Of human tradition, politic,
These truths broke through like morning light,
And scattered medieval night.
Still today they stand as true
As when the Reformers knew
That God's Word would forever stand,
Though heaven and earth should pass like sand.

THE TWO WAYS - INSPIRED BY PSALM 1

BLESSED IS THE MAN who walks not where
   The wicked tread with knowing sneer,
   Who turns his feet from paths that lead
   To scorners' seats and sinful deed.
   He stands not in the broad highway
   Where sinners pause to mock and bray,
   Nor plants himself among the proud
   Who jeer at God before the crowd.
   The counsel of the ungodly falls
   Like poison rain on listening souls.
   Their whispered schemes and plotting dark
   Leave conscience seared, leave deadly mark.
   But oh, the man whose chief delight
   Burns steady through both day and night
   In God's own law, that perfect word

Where truth rings clear and hope is heard.
He meditates when morning breaks,
He ponders when the evening wakes.
Not empty chanting, mindless drone,
But chewing truth like marrow from bone.
The law of God, his meat and drink,
The well from which he draws to think.
Each precept sweet upon his tongue,
Each promise like a battle song.
By day he walks with Scripture's light
Illuminating left and right.
By night upon his bed he turns
The holy words as his heart burns.
Like tree transplanted by the streams
Where water flows and sunlight gleams,
His roots run deep through fertile ground,
Where living water may be found.
The streams of God that never fail,
That flow through drought and bitter hail,
Supply the soul with secret strength
When trials come at any length.
He shall be like that blessed tree
Whose leaves stay green eternally.
Not autumn's curse nor winter's breath
Can bring those branches unto death.
In season comes the promised fruit,
Born from the life within the root.
Not forced or strained, but natural flow
From what the inner man does know.

Patient love and gentle peace,
Joy that brings the heart release,
Kindness, goodness, self-control,
The Spirit's fruit within the soul.
Whatever work his hand finds right,
Whatever task by day or night,
The Lord establishes his way
And prospers what he does each day.
Not that every scheme succeeds
Or that he never feels life's needs,
But deeper prosperity flows,
The kind that only heaven knows.
The wicked are not so at all,
But like the chaff before the squall.
No root, no weight, no solid core,
Just husks the wind sweeps off the floor.
When harvest time brings threshing severe,
The wheat remains, the chaff disappears.
The winnowing fork in the Master's hand
Divides the true from shifting sand.
They have no weight of character formed,
No substance when life's trials have stormed.
Like tumbleweeds across the plain,
They blow wherever they might gain.
Therefore, the wicked will not stand
When judgment comes across the land.
Their legs like water will give way
Before the Judge on that great day.
No clever argument or plea,

No hiding in the company
Of others who have played the fool,
Each stands alone before God's rule.
Nor shall the sinners find their place
Among the righteous in that space
Where God's own people gather round
And songs of victory resound.
The congregation of the just,
Those who in Christ have put their trust,
Will shine like stars forever bright
While sinners vanish into night.
For intimate knowledge marks the way,
The Lord knows His own night and day.
Not distant observation cold,
But tender love that will not fold.
He knows their rising and their rest,
Each secret struggle in the breast,
Each victory small, each battle won,
Each prayer lifted to the Son.
The Hebrew speaks of knowing deep,
The way a shepherd knows his sheep.
Not facts about, but relationship
That holds through every storm-tossed trip.
He knows the righteous, knows by name,
Has carved them on His palm for fame.
Through Christ, their Mediator true,
He sees them as the morning dew.
But oh, the pathway of the lost
Leads through the wasteland, tempest tossed.

No shepherd guards, no father waits,
Just empty, ever-darkening straits.
The way of the ungodly leads
Through thorns disguised as pleasant meadows.
What seems so right unto their eyes
Ends in destruction and demise.
They perish, not just bodies dying,
But souls forever classified
As those who chose the broader gate
And found too late their awful fate.
The road grows darker as they go,
Less light above, more dark below,
Until at last the path gives way
To everlasting death's decay.
Two men, two trees, two destinies,
The psalm paints clear for all who'd see.
No neutral ground on which to stand,
Just blessed or cursed from God's own hand.
Two ways diverge before each soul:
The narrow path that leads to whole,
The broad highway that crowds prefer
But ends where hope cannot occur.
Choose this day whom you will serve,
From which pathway you'll not swerve.
For every step confirms your choice
To heed or spurn the Spirit's voice.
The blessed man has made his stand,
God's Word his guide, God's law his land.
While storm winds blow the chaff away,

He stands unmoved till eternal day.

THE COVENANT THREAD

From Eden's dawn to glory's crown,
   One scarlet thread runs up and down
   Through every page of sacred writ,
   God's covenant, His holy grit.
   Not contracts cold that men devise
   With clauses, terms, and compromise,
   But bonds of blood and sovereign grace
   That span all time and every place.
   Before the stars learned how to shine,
   Before the planets fell in line,
   The Triune God in council met
   And covenant love forever set.
   The Father chose a people there,
   The Son agreed their curse to bear,
   The Spirit vowed to make them new,

Eternal pact between the Two.
This covenant of redemption made
Before foundation stones were laid
Secured salvation's mighty plan
Before God breathed and formed a man.
In Eden's garden, fresh and fair,
God placed the man He fashioned there.
Not left alone without a word,
But bound by covenant to his Lord.
The covenant of works stood clear:
Obey and live, rebel and fear.
The tree of knowledge marked the test,
Would Adam choose curse or be blessed?
Life promised to obedience true,
Death threatened disobedience too.
Not just for Adam standing there,
But all his seed that he would bear.
Federal headship was his role,
Representative of every soul
That would from him descend in time,
His glory theirs, or else his crime.
The woman came, the serpent spoke,
The covenant of works was broke.
One bite brought death to all mankind,
Left every soul condemned and blind.
But in that darkest hour of need,
God promised One from woman's seed
Would crush the serpent's wicked head,
Though His own heel would bruise and bleed.

ROOTED IN GRACE

The covenant of grace broke through,
As morning breaks with mercies new.
Not based on what mankind could do,
But Christ's own work, faithful and true.
To Noah next the promise came,
While flood waters cleansed earth's shame.
The rainbow arced across the sky,
God's covenant that earth won't die.
Common grace to all below,
Seasons come and harvests grow.
The sun and rain on just and wrong
Until the final judgment song.
Then Abraham heard God's own voice
Call him to make the hardest choice,
Leave everything he'd ever known
And trust the God he'd barely known.
The covenant signs were strange indeed:
Countless stars would match his seed,
The land of Canaan their inheritance,
And through his line, the world's deliverance.
Circumcision marked the sign,
Cut in flesh by God's design.
Every male child on the eighth day
Bore covenant marks that would not fade away.
But deeper than the outward knife,
God promised everlasting life
To all who shared Abraham's faith,
The substance underneath the wraith.
Through Isaac then the promise flowed,

Not Ishmael, though firstborn showed.
God's sovereign choice made crystal clear:
Not flesh but promise perseveres.
To Jacob next, the younger twin,
Despite his schemes and desperate sin.
The covenant blessing can't be earned,
Grace gives what merit never learned.
Four hundred years in Egypt's land,
The promise seemed like shifting sand.
But God remembered covenant made
And came in power to give them aid.
Through Moses next the law arrived,
Not so that they might be revived
From death to life by keeping rules,
The law served greater purpose tools.
The covenant at Sinai's height
Revealed God's holy, perfect right.
The moral law showed God's own heart,
What holiness required from the start.
Ceremonial laws portrayed
The coming sacrifice Christ made.
Each lamb upon the altar spoke
Of Him whose death would bear sin's yoke.
Civil laws for Israel's state,
To make them separate and great.
A holy nation set apart
To show the world God's very heart.
But still the covenant of grace
Flowed underneath, the centerplace.

For all the law could ever do
Was show what sin had twisted through.
The law served as a tutor strict
To show how deeply man was sick.
No healing in the law was found,
Just diagnosis of the wound.
It drove the burdened souls to see
Their only hope was mercy free.
The sacrifices year by year
Could never take away sin's fear.
King David next received the word:
His throne would last, thus saith the Lord.
Through David's line would come a King
Whose reign would never cease or dim.
The covenant with David made
Pointed to that coming day
When David's greater Son would reign
Over earth's entire domain.
Through prophets then the picture grew
More detailed and more glorious too.
A new covenant was coming near,
Written on hearts, not stones severe.
Jeremiah saw that promised day
When God would take their hearts of clay
And make them soft to His commands,
Not by their might, but by His hands.
The law once written on cold stone
Would find its true and living home
Inside the hearts of all His people,

From least to greatest, under heaven's steeple.
When Christ arrived, the time was full,
The shadows met their substance.
Every promise found its Yes
In Him who came our souls to bless.
He kept the covenant of works complete,
Never did His footsteps retreat
From perfect righteousness each day,
The life of obedience on display.
Then to the cross the Savior went
As covenant Mediator sent.
The federal Head of all His own,
He died for sins not His alone.
His blood established the new covenant promised,
Every ancient longing accomplished.
Better promises on better ground,
Where grace, not law, would now abound.
The church was born, Jew and Gentile one,
No dividing wall when God's work's done.
The olive tree of covenant blessing
Spread its branches, all confessing.
Baptism replaced the bloody knife,
Water speaking death to life.
The covenant sign to every nation,
Male and female in salvation.
The Supper too spoke covenant truth,
Christ's body broken for His youth,
His blood poured out to seal the deal,
Making all the promises real.

ROOTED IN GRACE

One covenant of grace remains
Through all the Bible's varied refrains.
Different administrations true,
But same salvation through and through.
From Adam's fall to glory's door,
One people God is calling for.
One faith, one hope, one Christ to save
From Eden's loss to past the grave.
The saints of old looked forward still
To Christ who would God's promise fill.
We now look back at Calvary's tree
Where covenant blood set sinners free.
Reformed theology holds this thread,
By grace alone we're comforted.
In Christ alone our Head we find,
The second Adam of mankind.
Through faith alone we take our stand,
Not works performed by human hand.
Scripture alone reveals the way
This covenant works yesteryear and today.
For God's glory alone the plan unfolds,
As covenant promise takes hold.
From eternities past to ages unending,
Grace and truth in Christ transcending.

THE THRONE ABOVE ALL THRONES

BEFORE THE MOUNTAINS LEARNED to rise,
  Before the first star lit the skies,
  Before the word "Let there be" rang,
  God ruled supreme, no challenge sprang.
  His sovereignty needs no defense,
  No vote to grant Him competence.
  He sits enthroned, was always there,
  Beyond all time, beyond compare.
  The Reformed faith holds this truth dear:
  God governs all, both far and near.
  No maverick molecule runs free,
  No atom spins outside His decree.
  From quantum realm to galaxy wide,
  His sovereign will cannot be denied.
  The sparrow falls, He marks its place,

ROOTED IN GRACE

The mighty empires know His grace.
Consider how the Scripture speaks
Of God's control from peaks to creeks.
"Whatever the Lord pleases, He does"
Not merely wishes, dreams, or was.
In heaven high and earth below,
In seas profound where darkness flows,
His sovereignty extends complete,
No realm exists His rule can't meet.
He works all things, yes, all, take note,
According to His will devote.
Not some things, most things, many things,
But all beneath His sovereign wings.
The heart of kings rests in His hand,
Like water channels through the land,
He turns them wheresoever He wills,
His purposes alone fulfills.
When Nebuchadnezzar boasted loud,
His kingdom strong, his heart so proud,
God humbled him to eat like cattle,
Showed who truly wins each battle.
"The Most High rules in kingdoms here,
Gives them to whomever He holds dear."
The mighty king learned through his shame
That earthly power's just a game.
Compared to Him who rules above,
Whose sovereignty flows from His love,
All nations are but drops that fall
From buckets, He outlasts them all.

The lot is cast into the lap,
But every decision's in His map.
What seems like chance to human eyes
Flows from His sovereign enterprise.
He raises kings and tears them down,
Bestows and then removes the crown.
The times and seasons in His grip,
No schedule from His hand can slip.
This sovereignty's no distant thing,
Detached and cold, a heartless king.
It pulses with His perfect love,
Each sovereign act fits like a glove.
Around His children's every need,
His sovereign care plants every seed.
He numbers hairs upon our heads,
Provides our daily bread.
The Reformed tradition clearly sees
God's rule over human pleas.
Free will exists, but not supreme,
It flows within His sovereign stream.
We choose what we desire most,
But He's the sovereign, gracious host
Who shapes desires, bends the will,
Yet leaves us choosing freely still.
Like Joseph told his brothers who
Had sold him into slavery's hue:
"You meant it evil, but God meant good"
Both wills accomplished where they stood.
The cross displays this mystery bright:

Wicked hands brought darkest night,
Yet God's determined plan before
Accomplished what He'd purposed for.
Judas chose with evil heart,
Played his self-selected part.
Yet Jesus said it had to be,
Sovereign plan and human decree.
His sovereignty brings comfort deep
To those who trust Him with their sleep.
No accident can break His plan,
No surprise disrupts His hand.
When cancer comes or children stray,
When darkness seems to own the day,
The sovereign God still holds the throne,
We're never left to walk alone.
He's working all things for the good
Of those who love Him as they should.
Not all things are good in themselves alone,
But He makes all things serve His own.
The tapestry from underneath
Shows tangled threads like dragon's teeth.
But from above, His sovereign view
Reveals the pattern pure and true.
In suffering, His sovereignty
Doesn't mean He's the enemy.
The God who spared not His own Son
But gave Him up for everyone,
How shall He not with Him also
Freely give us all we need to grow?

His sovereignty serves love's great end,
On this His children can depend.
Election flows from sovereign choice,
Not merit found in human voice.
Before the world's foundation laid,
His sovereign love the selection made.
Not based on foreseen faith or deed,
But sovereign grace alone decreed
That some from Adam's fallen race
Would know His sovereign, saving grace.
This doctrine humbles human pride,
No boasting can with truth reside.
If God is sovereign in salvation,
Then grace alone heals our damnation.
The wind blows where it wishes free,
You hear its sound through field and tree,
But cannot tell from whence it came,
So sovereign Spirit works the same.
In providence, His sovereign hand
Upholds the sea, sustains the land.
By Him all things consist and hold,
His power never growing old.
Each heartbeat happens by His will,
Each breath He grants is sovereign still.
In Him we live and move and have
Our being, sovereign grace like salve.
The weather patterns, rain and drought,
He sends them in or holds them out.
No storm surprises Him with force,

He guides the hurricane's course.
The nations rage, they plot in vain,
Against the Lord's Anointed reign.
He laughs, not cruel but knowing well
Their schemes against Him cannot quell.
His sovereign purpose standing fast,
From ages past to ages last.
The Lamb was slain before time started,
His sovereign plan never departed.
Even evil serves His ends,
Though never are they allies or friends.
He permits what He could prevent,
For purposes magnificent.
Like Luther's mighty hymn declared:
"The prince of darkness grim, we trailed not him.
His rage we can endure,
For lo! his doom is sure,
One little word shall fell him."
That word flows from the sovereign throne,
Where God has never sat alone.
The Trinity in perfect unity
Rules with sovereign community.
This doesn't make us puppets dancing,
Strings pulled tight at His commanding.
His sovereignty established free
The will He gave to you and me.
Mystery? Yes, but not contradiction.
Bible holds this truth conviction:
God is sovereign, man responsible.

Both truths are biblically possible.
The Reformed faith refuses neat
And tidy systems that compete
With Scripture's both and testimony.
We bow before the mystery.
His thoughts are higher than our thoughts,
His ways than ours by infinite lots.
The finite cannot comprehension gain
Of infinite's sovereign domain.
Yet what's revealed belongs to us,
In these revealed truths we trust:
God reigns supreme over all creation,
Working out His preservation.
Of all His saints through time and space,
By sovereign, free, and matchless grace.
No purpose of His can be stopped,
No plan of His has ever flopped.
Take comfort then, you blood-bought church,
You're held by Him who cannot lurch
From throne to throne uncertain, weak,
He's sovereign God of whom we speak!
From eternity past He chose your name,
Through time He called you to His fame,
To eternity future you'll adore
The sovereign God forevermore.

THE HEAVENS DECLARE - INSPIRED BY PSALM 19

The sky stretched out like parchment vast,
   Each star a letter spelling fast
   The glory of the God who made
   Both blazing sun and cooling shade.
   No language spoken, yet they preach,
   The galaxies in spiral reach
   Proclaim their Maker's power true,
   While morning breaks with mercied dew.
   From east to west the sun runs course,
   A bridegroom strong, rejoicing force.
   Nothing hidden from its heat,
   God's faithfulness in circuit complete.
   The cosmos shouts what hearts resist:
   That God alone does truly exist.

In majesty beyond compare,
Creation's voice fills everywhere.
Yet greater still than starlit night,
Than canyon deep or mountain height,
The law of God speaks clearer truth
To aged saint and searching youth.
The Word more fixed than Polaris bright,
More sure than gravity's downward flight.
When scientists revise their claim,
God's promises remain the same.
"The law of the LORD is perfect," sang
The shepherd king, whose harp strings rang
With truths that pierce the modern soul
As surely as they made him whole.
Converting souls, not merely minds,
The Word breaks through what culture blinds.
Total depravity's dark spell
Cannot resist when God speaks well.
The testimony sure and right,
Makes simple ones learn wisdom's sight.
Not human wisdom, proud and vain,
But truth that flows from God's domain.
The statutes of the LORD rejoice
The heart that hears His sovereign voice.
Not burdensome but sweet release,
His yoke brings rest, His burden peace.
The commandment pure enlightens eyes
That once saw only earth and skies.
Now heaven breaks through nature's veil,

And grace writes its eternal tale.
More to be desired than gold,
Than much fine gold the psalmist told.
What Wall Street chases, what kingdoms hoard,
Pales next to one verse from the Lord.
Sweeter than honey from the comb,
His words call prodigals back home.
The taste that satisfies completely,
While worldly pleasures fade so fleetly.
By them Your servant finds his warning.
Danger flags for each new morning.
The guardrails on the narrow way
That keep the pilgrim's feet from stray.
In keeping them lies great reward,
Not wages earned but grace out poured.
Obedience flows from gratitude's spring,
Not servile fear of punishment's sting.
But who can understand his errors?
The heart holds depths of hidden terrors.
Cleanse me from my secret faults,
The ones that hide in memory's vaults.
The sins I've rationalized away,
The compromises made each day.
The pride dressed up as confidence,
The greed disguised as providence.
Keep back Your servant from presumptuous sins,
Those bold rebellions where destruction wins.
Let them not have dominion's power,
Be Lord of every thought and hour.

Then shall I be upright and clean,
Innocent of transgression's scheme.
Not by my work but by Your grace,
Covered by Christ's righteousness, embrace.
David knew what Calvin taught:
That every good in us is wrought
By God alone who works within
To will and do despite our sin.
The psalm now turns to meditation,
From cosmic shout to contemplation.
Let the words my mouth would speak,
And every thought that makes me weak
Or strong, or anywhere between,
Be acceptable and clean
Before You, LORD, my strength, my rock,
The God who hears before I talk.
My Redeemer, blood-bought name!
The psalm ends where gospel came.
From stars to law to grace's plea,
Creation sings soteriology.
The heavens declare, the Word makes known,
But only Christ can bring us home.
The threefold cord that can't be broken:
God's world, God's Word, God's Son has spoken.
This Reformed truth the psalm contains:
That common grace through nature reigns,
But special revelation's light
Alone makes saving knowledge bright.
The skeptic sees the Milky Way

But explains its dance away.
The believer sees and hearing, hears
The music of the spheres.
For those with eyes opened by grace,
Each sunset shows the Father's face.
Each thunderstorm displays His power,
Each gentle rain, His mercy's shower.
But nature's book, though clearly writ,
Cannot the soul from sin acquit.
It renders all without excuse
But cannot break sin's binding noose.
We need the Scriptures' clearer voice,
To understand the Father's choice,
To know the Son who came to save,
To feel the Spirit's power brave.
The Westminster divines declared
What Psalm Nineteen always shared:
That God's existence, power, and glory
Nature tells, but not salvation's story.
The fool says in his heart, "No God"
While standing on the earth He trod,
Breathing air that He sustains,
Rebelling with God-given brains.
But we who've tasted grace's wine,
Who've felt His sovereign love divine,
We see His fingerprints everywhere:
In ocean depth and mountain air.
In DNA's complex code,
In every creature's set abode,

In laws of physics, fixed and true,
In morning's ever-mercied dew.
Yet we treasure more His Word,
Where clearest truth is ever heard.
Where Christ steps from each sacred page,
God's final Word for every age.
The heavens declare His glory bright,
But Scripture shows His saving might.
Both books are His, both books are true,
But only one makes all things new.
So let this be our daily prayer,
As we breathe God's common grace air:
That words and thoughts would honor Him
Who lit the stars and conquers sin.
Our strength when we are weak and worn,
Our rock when faith seems hardly born,
Our Redeemer when we fall,
The God who's sovereign over all.

Christ Crushes Satan - Inspired by Psalm 110

The LORD declared to David's Lord,
   Strange words that rang prophetic chord.
   "Sit at My right hand in power,
   Until I make Your foes to cower."
Two Lords in one divine decree,
The Trinity's own mystery.
The Father speaks to Christ the Son,
Before all time their war was won.
"Your enemies," not Mine alone,
But those who rage against Your throne.
For Father, Son, and Spirit share
One enemy they'll not long spare.
A footstool for Your conquering feet,
Their judgment sure, their doom complete.

Not equals battling for the crown,
But rebels who will be cast down.
Calvin saw what moderns miss:
No dualism dwells in this.
Satan never was God's peer,
Just a creature ruled by fear.
The serpent's head already crushed
When Christ from Joseph's tomb was raised.
Though still he writhes in death's last throes,
His fate was sealed at Calvary's close.
The LORD sends forth from Zion's hill
Your mighty scepter, sovereign will.
Rule in the midst of all Your foes!
The kingdom comes despite who oppose.
Not waiting for some future day
When opposition melts away.
Christ rules now among His enemies,
Converting rebels to their knees.
Each salvation tells the story:
Satan robbed of stolen glory.
Every prayer prayed in Jesus' name
Puts the ancient foe to shame.
Your people shall be volunteers,
Free-willing through their joyful tears.
In the day of Your great power,
In that soul-awakening hour.
Not forced against their captive will,
But drawn by grace irresistible.
What seemed like choice was sovereign call,

The gift of faith that conquers all.
In holy garments, priestly-dressed,
Your people come to find their rest.
From the womb of morning's birth,
Like dew, You have Your youth on earth.
Fresh mercies with each rising sun,
New converts till the age is done.
The church forever young though old,
Because her Lord will not grow cold.
The LORD has sworn, His oath secure,
His covenant forever sure:
"You are a priest eternally
After Melchizedek's decree."
Not Aaron's line that failed and fell,
But One who conquers death and hell.
Both king and priest in one divine,
Pouring out both bread and wine.
No temple made with human hands
Could hold the One who heaven commands.
His priesthood needs no blood of goats,
His own blood better covenant wrote.
The Lord stands ready at Your right,
Reversing roles in sovereign might.
He'll shatter kings in wrath's great day
When patience gives to judgment way.
The kings who said, "Let's break their bands,
And cast their cords from off our hands."
Who raged against the LORD's Anointed,
Will find their rebellion disappointed.

He judges nations, fills with slain,
Not random violence, but justice's reign.
The corpses piled are mercy's end
For those who would not bow but bend.
He crushes heads throughout the land,
The serpent's seed on every hand.
From Eden's curse to final fight,
The woman's Seed sets all things right.
But pause, what picture interrupts?
"He drinks from brooks" the scene disrupts
Our vision of the Warrior King
To show a very human thing.
The One who rules at God's right hand
Still walked our dust, still touched our land.
True God, true man, the creed's confession
Lived out in brook-side intercession.
He thirsted so we'd never thirst,
He died that we might be dispersed
From death's dominion, Satan's claim,
To glory in His matchless name.
Therefore He lifts His head on high,
Not pride but victory's battle cry.
The suffering servant now exalted,
The humble One no more assaulted.
This psalm that Jesus used to teach
When Pharisees stood within reach,
"How can David call Him Lord
If He's his son?" The living Word
Confounded those who would not see

Two natures in one majesty.
The son of David, David's Lord,
Both root and branch in sweet accord.
Satan heard these words and trembled,
Knowing all his lies dissembled.
The seed of woman prophesied
Would be the One he crucified.
He thought the cross his greatest hour,
His masterpiece of hellish power.
But resurrection's dawn revealed
His doom was thereby signed and sealed.
For every temptation overcome,
Each sinless word from Jesus' tongue,
Each miracle that broke sin's chain
Proclaimed that Satan would not reign.
The strong man bound, his house now plundered,
His captives freed, his kingdom sundered.
Christ leads captivity captive high,
While Satan's hosts can only cry.
Yet still the dragon makes his war
Against the church on earth's far shore.
He knows his time is short and fleet,
He knows he faces sure defeat.
But rage drives him to persecute
The woman and her offspring's fruit.
He cannot touch the throne above,
So strikes at those whom Jesus loves.
The martyrs' blood through history spilled,
The faithful saints by tyrants killed,

Each one a footstool being made,
Each death a stone in victory's grade.
For what the serpent cannot see,
Blinded by his enmity,
Is every saint who dies in faith
Destroys more of his kingdom's wraith.
The church advances through her pain,
Her losses become Satan's bane.
Where one falls, ten rise up instead,
The gospel spreads though saints lie dead.
Reformed theology makes it plain:
Christ rules now, not will reign.
The kingdom came when He arose,
And daily conquers all His foes.
Not waiting for some future date
To exercise His kingly state.
He sits enthroned at God's right hand,
And nothing thwarts what He has planned.
The footstool-making carries on
From that first Easter Sunday dawn.
Each day brings Satan lower still,
Each convert breaks his weakening will.
Until that final day arrives
When none of Satan's host survives.
When every knee bows, tongue confesses,
And Christ His enemies suppresses.
The last enemy is death itself,
That ancient thief of human health.
But death died when Christ arose,

The grave became His conquered foes.
Then Satan, death, and hades all
Into the lake of fire fall.
The footstool-making is complete,
All enemies beneath His feet.
But now, today, the battle rages,
Though we know how ends the ages.
We fight from victory, not for it,
The conquered foe can only forfeit.
So when the darkness seems to win,
When Satan's lies come flooding in,
Remember Christ sits throned above,
And rules His kingdom through His love.
The serpent's head bears crushing weight,
His doom is sealed, though seems he great.
Christ Jesus rules from heaven's throne,
And Satan cannot shake His own.

The Gospel in the Garden - Inspired by Genesis 3 and the Belgic Confession Article 17

Before the world heard thunder roll,
   Before the law carved stone made whole,
   Before the prophets raised their cry,
   Before the Baptist's voice soared high,
   The gospel bloomed in Eden's shame,
   When sin and death first staked their claim.
   Not in the Temple's holy place,
   But where the serpent showed his face,
   Where innocence lay crushed and broken,
   The first good news was clearly spoken.
   Genesis three, that darkest hour,

When mankind fell to Satan's power.
The woman reached, she took, she ate,
And sealed humanity's dire fate.
Her husband stood beside her there,
Silent guardian of despair.
He took the fruit from rebel hands,
And broke the Lord's direct commands.
Their eyes flew open, not to see
The godhood promised cunningly,
But nakedness and shame laid bare,
And terror in the evening air.
They heard His footsteps in the cool,
The God they'd treated as a fool.
Among the trees they tried to hide.
As if omniscience could be denied.
"Where are you?" called the sovereign Lord,
Not ignorance but grace out poured.
He drew them out despite their shame,
To speak the curse and speak His name.
The man blamed God and blamed his wife,
The woman blamed the serpent's strife.
But neither took upon their head
The weight of what they'd done and said.
Then justice spoke to each in turn,
The serpent first would feel the burn:
"Upon your belly you shall go,
And dust shall be your food below."
But tucked within that curse divine,
A promise broke through judgment's line:

"I'll put an enmity," God said,
"Between your seed and woman's seed.
He'll crush your head beneath His heel,
Though you His heel shall bruise with zeal."
The Belgic speaks with clarity,
Article seventeen's decree:
"We believe that our most gracious God,
In His admirable wisdom stood
And goodness, seeing that man
Had thrown himself by Satan's plan
Into physical and spiritual death,
And made himself with every breath
Wholly miserable, was pleased to seek
And comfort him when he did sneak
Trembling from His presence high,
And promising him that He
Would give His Son, born of a woman,
To bruise the head of Satan's scheming,
And would make him happy."
See the glory in this story,
God pursued when man retreated,
God spoke hope when man lay defeated.
Not because of human merit,
But from grace they would inherit
Life from death and joy from sorrow,
Light to shine in shame's tomorrow.
The woman heard her sentence read:
Pain in childbirth, tears she'd shed.
Desire for her husband's rule,

While he would often play the fool.
Yet in that curse shone golden thread,
She'd bear the One to crush the head.
Through labor pains and sweat and blood,
Through generations' rolling flood,
Her daughters would keep bearing sons
Until the promised day would come.
When virgin's womb would hold the Lord,
The woman's seed, the Living Word.
No human father's contribution,
Just divine substitution.
The Spirit overshadowed Mary,
That the Seed be pure, not ordinary.
To Adam came the hardest blow:
"By sweat of brow your food you'll grow.
The ground will fight you all your days,
Thorns and thistles block your ways.
Until you return unto the dust,
For die you must, yes, die you must."
The very ground from which he came
Would swallow him in death and shame.
His labor turned from joy to toil,
His harvest mixed with cursed soil.
Yet even here grace intervened,
Not instant death as might have been.
But time to work and wait and yearn
For promised Seed to make return.
And then the Lord did something strange,
He killed an animal to arrange

A covering for their nakedness,
The first blood shed for human mess.
Those skins spoke louder than mere words:
That sin meant death, that blood conferred
A covering for their guilty frame,
That God Himself bore all the blame.
For who else could have prevented
What the serpent had invented?
Who else could have stayed the hand
That reached to take what He had banned?
Yet sovereign wisdom had decreed
To let the woman take and feed,
To demonstrate before all eyes
That only grace could make them wise.
The Gospel in the Garden grew
From blood-soaked ground and morning dew.
Not plan B or backup course,
But always God's intended source
Of glory both for Him and man,
The cross foreshadowed in His plan.
Before the world's foundation stone,
The Lamb was slain, His fate foreknown.
So when we read of Eden's fall,
We're reading grace that conquers all.
When we see our first parents' shame,
We see why Jesus came.
The garden's gospel still rings true,
That God pursues both me and you.
That in our hiding, He still calls,

That grace catches us when we fall.
That though we merit only death,
He gives His Son with every breath.
The woman's Seed has crushed the snake,
Though bruised He was for our sake.
The second Adam has undone
What first Adam had begun.
Where Eden's tree brought death and curse,
Calvary's tree did both reverse.
Where Adam failed the test divine,
Christ Jesus passed through every line.
Reformed theology holds this dear,
That all was planned before time's sphere.
The fall permitted, not desired,
That grace might be the more admired.
For how could mercy show its face
Without a need for saving grace?
How could justice demonstrate
Its perfection pure and great
Unless there was rebellion deep
For holy wrath to sow and reap?
But then how could God's love be known
In all its height and breadth full-grown
Unless He gave His only Son
To save the vile and undone?
The Garden's gospel still speaks true
To every sinner, me and you:
That God seeks those who hide in shame,
That He clothes those who bear the blame,

That though the curse is just and real,
The promise makes the broken heal.
For every daughter of Eve who weeps,
For every son of Adam who reaps
The whirlwind of their ancient choice,
Listen to the Gospel's voice:
"The Seed has come, the Head is crushed,
The serpent's accusations hushed.
Come out from hiding in your shame,
Be clothed in righteousness through His name."

The Pattern of All Prayer - Inspired by the Lord's Prayer

Our Father, not a distant force,
   Not cosmic consciousness or source,
   But, Father, personal and near,
   To all His children, bought so dear.
   In heaven, seated on the throne,
   Above all powers earth has known,
   Sovereign over time and space,
   Ruling all by sovereign grace.
   Hallowed be Your name, set apart,
   Sacred truth in every heart.
   Not empty words or ritual said,
   But reverence that bows the head.
   Your kingdom come, that blessed reign
   Where righteousness alone sustains,

Where Christ rules with iron rod
O'er all the enemies of God.
Already here, but not yet full,
The kingdom's power to push and pull.
In hearts where Christ has made His home,
Yet waiting still for Him to come.
Your will be done, not ours, we pray,
Though flesh rebels and turns away.
Your will, so perfect, good, and right,
Our sanctification's light.
On earth as heaven, no divide
Between the realms where You preside.
Your will obeyed without delay
By angels bright as earthen clay.
Give us this day our daily bread,
Not stones for children who've been fed
The Bread of Life, broken, torn,
That they might never hunger mourn.
Both physical and spiritual food,
All provisions for our good.
Dependent creatures, we confess,
Looking to You for every bless.
Forgive our debts, impossible plea
Apart from Calvary's crimson tree.
Ten thousand talents owed Your name,
Paid in full through Jesus' shame.
As we forgive our debtors too,
Not earning pardon, but made new,
We show the grace we've been shown,

Forgiving as we've been forgiven.
Reformed hearts knew this truth so well:
Forgiveness flowed from grace's swell.
Not the cause but evidence
Of hearts transformed by providence.
Lead us not into temptation,
Sovereign over every station,
You test but never tempt to sin,
You guard the souls You've gathered in.
But deliver us from evil,
From the world, flesh, and the devil.
Three enemies that wage their war
Against the souls You've ransomed for.
The evil one, that ancient snake,
Who prowls about for souls to take.
But greater He who dwells within
Than all the powers of hell and sin.
For Yours the kingdom, none can steal
What You've determined under seal.
No rival throne can stand or last,
Your kingdom's die forever cast.
And Yours the power, unlimited,
Never waning or diminished.
Omnipotent to save and keep
Your chosen ones, Your precious sheep.
And Yours the glory, ultimate end
To which all creatures must descend.
All things exist to show Your worth,
In heaven above and here on earth.

Forever and ever, without end,
No seasons change or shadows bend.
Eternal God, eternally praised,
By souls from death forever raised.
Amen, so let it be,
This prayer of those set free.
Not magic words or mystic spell,
But pattern Christ gave us to tell.
Each petition rightly prayed
By those the Spirit had remade.
Not vain repetition's empty sound,
But depths where living faith was found.
The Lord's Prayer in Reformed light
Shone with predestination's might.
Each phrase a window to behold
The doctrines of grace, more precious than gold.

The Ancient Declaration - Inspired by the Apostles' Creed

I BELIEVE IN GOD the Father, first word strikes
   Like hammer blow on anvil, sparks that fly
   From metal shaped by sovereign hands. Not "we"
   But "I" each soul must stand alone before
   The throne of grace, must make confession real.
   No proxy faith, no borrowed light suffices
   When darkness presses close and doubts assail.
   The Father, not abstract philosophy
   Or prime unmover distant from His work,
   But, Father, choosing children ere the world
   Began its spinning dance through time and space.
   Election's love preceded our first breath,

Adoption papers signed in blood divine
Before the morning stars sang their first song.
Almighty, power without limit, force
That spoke and galaxies sprang into being,
That numbers every hair and knows each sparrow's
Fall to earth. No maverick molecules
Escape His sovereign rule, no random chance
Disturbs the purpose of His perfect will.
From quantum realm to cosmic sweep, He reigns.
Maker of heaven and earth, the visible
And invisible, principalities
And powers bow before creative Word.
Ex nihilo, from nothing into glory,
The universe unfolds at His command.
Not deist clockmaker who winds and leaves,
But intimate sustainer, moment by moment
Upholding all things by His powerful word.
And in Jesus Christ, the hinge on which
All history turns, the center point
Of revelation. Not mere teacher, prophet,
Revolutionary or example good,
But God incarnate, second Adam, come
To win what first Adam lost through pride.
The God-man, dual nature unified.
His only Son, unique, begotten not
Created, of same substance with the Father,
Light from Light and very God from God.
Eternal generation's mystery,
The Son forever flowing from the Father

Yet never diminished, never separate.
Monogenes, the one and only One.
Our Lord, not just Savior but Master too,
Not fire insurance from hell's flame
But sovereign ruler over every inch
Of life redeemed. The Heidelberg spoke true:
"I am not my own but belong, body
And soul, in life and death, to Jesus Christ."
No compartments secular remain.
Conceived by the Holy Spirit, miracle
That skeptics mock but faith adores. The Word
Made flesh without a human father's seed,
The Spirit overshadowing virgin womb.
No taint of Adam's sin passed down through blood,
The Second Adam came immaculate,
Prepared to be the spotless Lamb of God.
Born of the Virgin Mary, scandal to
The Greeks who sought their wisdom, stumbling block
To Jews who wanted signs. Young peasant girl,
Perhaps fourteen, chosen vessel for
The hope of ages. Not perpetual
Virgin as Rome contends, but faithful servant
Who bore the Christ and other children too.
Suffered under Pontius Pilate, history
Invades the creed with the Roman procurator's name.
Not myth or legend but dated fact,
When Tiberius Caesar held the throne
And Herod played at kingship. Real wood,
Real nails, real blood that flowed from opened veins.

The suffering servant Isaiah saw.
Was crucified, the slave's death, cursed tree,
Where wrath of God met love of God in cosmic
Clash that shook the earth and tore the veil.
Propitiation's work accomplished there,
The cup of fury drained to bitter dregs
By Him who knew no sin but was made sin
That we might be the righteousness of God.
Dead and buried, no swoon theory here,
No partial payment for an infinite debt.
The Roman spear made certain, blood and water
Flowed from pierced side. Joseph's tomb received
The corpse of God. Death died when Life expired,
The grave would learn it could not hold its prey,
But for three days the body lay in darkness.
He descended into hell, or to the dead,
Debate has raged through centuries of thought.
Not suffering more but proclaiming triumph
To spirits imprisoned, victory cry
That echoed through the realms below: "It's finished!"
The strong man bound, his captives set free,
The keys of death and Hades claimed as spoils.
The third day He rose again, not metaphor
For hope renewed or memory that lingers,
But flesh and bone made new, scars still visible,
Eating fish with stunned disciples, breathing
Peace on those who'd fled. The firstfruits of
The resurrection harvest yet to come,
Death's conqueror with heel on serpent's head.

He ascended into heaven, forty days
Of teaching kingdom truths to slow hearts,
Then clouds received Him from their watching eyes.
Not abandonment but coronation,
The Son of man receiving dominion,
All authority in heaven and earth
Now given to the risen Lord of all.
Sits at the right hand, position of honor,
Of power, of intercession without ceasing.
Our advocate when Satan stands accusing,
Our high priest who sympathizes with
Our weaknesses, touched by our infirmities.
The session of the King who rules and reigns
Till every enemy lies beneath His feet.
From there He shall come, not might or could
But shall, as certain as the sunrise, sure
As breath. The blessed hope of His appearing,
When clouds roll back and trumpet sounds the call
And every eye beholds Him. Some with joy
Inexpressible, some with terror knowing
Too late the truth they spent their lives denying.
To judge the living and the dead, the court
Where no appeals exist, no lawyers plead,
Where books are opened and the secrets hidden
In darkness come to light. The sheep divided
From the goats, the wheat from tares, the final
Separation. Justice perfect meted out
By Him who bore injustice in our place.
I believe in the Holy Spirit, third person

Of the Trinity, not force or feeling
But God himself, who hovered over waters
At creation's dawn, who overshadowed
Mary's womb, who fell at Pentecost
Like fire and wind. The Comforter who leads
Into all truth, who quickens dead hearts.
The holy catholic church, not Roman institution
But universal body of believers,
The called-out ones from every tribe and tongue.
Invisible yet visible, triumphant
Yet militant, already but not yet.
The bride being prepared for wedding feast,
Still spotted, wrinkled, but being sanctified.
The communion of saints, that mystic union
Binding believers across time and space.
The church in heaven cheers the church on earth,
We stand with Abel, walk with Enoch, fight
With David, sing with Mary. Death no barrier
To fellowship of those in Christ. One body
With many members, each one precious, needed.
The forgiveness of sins, not mere forgetting
But judicial declaration: "Not guilty!"
Based on Another's merit, alien
Righteousness imputed to our account.
The double transfer: our sin laid on Him,
His perfection credited to us.
Amazing exchange that mercy wrought.
The resurrection of the body, not escape
From flesh but flesh redeemed, made glorious.

These very bodies, sown in weakness, raised
In power. Continuity yet transformation,
Like seed becoming tree yet still the same.
Creation groans for this revealing, when
The sons of God shine forth like stars.
The life everlasting, not mere duration
But quality of life that starts at new birth
And flowers into fullness at the end.
To know the only true God and Jesus Christ
Whom He has sent. Not harps on clouds but new
Creation's glory, work without futility,
Rest without boredom, joy without alloy.
Amen, so be it, let it stand,
This ancient creed that martyrs signed with blood,
That mothers whispered to their nursing babes,
That missionaries carried across oceans.
Not dead tradition but living truth,
Each line a battleground where heresy
Met orthodoxy and orthodoxy won.
The Apostles' Creed in Reformed light
Glowed with doctrines of electing grace.
Not bare minimum of belief but framework
For meditation deep on truths that shape
The soul and strengthen faith. Each phrase a door
Into the mysteries of redemption,
Each word a stone in truth's foundation sure.

The Tablets of Sinai: A Reformed Meditation

The mountain smoked. The trumpet blast grew louder,
   Longer, piercing desert air with sound
   No human lips had formed. The people cowered
   At Sinai's base while Moses climbed holy ground.
   Not arbitrary rules from cosmic tyrant
   But character of God carved into stone,
   The moral law that angels keep, aspirant
   To perfection that belongs to God alone.
   "You shall have no other gods before Me"
   The first and foundational word that sets
   All others into place. Not plural "we"
   But singular devotion God begets.
   The human heart, that idol factory,
   Forever crafting gods from wood and dream,

From money, sex, and power's mastery,
From comfort's lull and pleasure's fleeting gleam.
Reformed hearts knew this battle well, the fight
Against the subtle idols of the age:
Self-righteousness dressed up as moral right,
Good works performed on merit's empty stage.
Total depravity means every part
Corrupted, bent toward self-worship's shrine.
Only sovereign grace can turn the heart
From idols back to worship the Divine.
"You shall not make for yourself a carved image"
Not just of wood or stone but mental construct,
Tame deity that fits our lineage,
Our prejudice and preference. We're instructed
Here that God defines Himself, not we.
The golden calf still beckons in new forms:
The god who only loves, who cannot see
Our sin, who never judges, never storms.
The Reformers fought this battle hard and long
Against the icons and the Virgin's crown,
Against the saints' statues and pilgrim's song,
Stripping churches bare and tearing down
Whatever stood between the soul and God,
Whatever mediator save the Son.
The regulative principle their rod
And staff: worship only as God's Word has done.
"You shall not take the name of the LORD in vain"
More than just profanity eschewed,
But bearing God's name falsely, bringing stain

Upon His reputation. Those renewed
By grace must guard their witness carefully.
The hypocrite who Sunday morning sings
Then Monday morning cheats transparently
Does violence to holy, sacred things.
Calvin knew this weight, how those who claim
The name of Christ yet live in open sin
Cause enemies to blaspheme that name,
Make mockery of grace that dwells within.
Cheap grace that Bonhoeffer would decry,
Forgiveness without change, without the cross,
Takes God's name vainly, living out a lie
That turns the pearl of gospel into dross.
"Remember the Sabbath day, to keep it holy"
Creation's rhythm written in our frame,
One day in seven set apart wholly
For rest and worship, kindling again the flame
Of wonder at our Maker's works and ways.
The Puritans guarded Sunday strict and stern,
Not legalism but love-filled praise
For resurrection day, when we learn
To cease our striving, rest in finished work.
The Reformed tradition saw this day as gift,
Foretaste of eternal rest where lurk
No Monday deadlines. Here the soul can lift
Above the weekly grind and market's roar
To feast on Word and sacrament, to sing
With saints, remember what we're living for:
The glory of our Prophet, Priest, and King.

"Honor your father and your mother" first
Command with promise, Paul would later note.
The family unit, blessed or cursed,
Shapes souls for good or ill. The antidote
To generation's curse is honor paid
To those God placed in authority,
Even when their feet of clay have made
Deep wounds. The fifth commandment's guarantee:
Long life upon the land. But deeper still,
It speaks of order God built into life,
Authority and submission to His will
In every sphere. Not doormat under knife
But recognition that God rules through means,
Through parents, teachers, magistrates, and more.
The Reformed saw here what Scripture leans
Toward everywhere: God's sovereignty at core.
"You shall not murder" Jesus pressed this deeper:
Anger nursed in heart is murder's seed.
The Westminster divines, those careful keeper
Of doctrine, taught that we must also feed
The hungry, clothe the naked, visit those
In prison. Not just negative command
But positive: preserve life, oppose
Whatever would destroy what God has planned.
The image-bearer's life has sacred worth
Not from his merit, achievement, or race,
But from his Maker who brought him to birth
And stamped on him indelible His face.
"You shall not commit adultery" covenant

Breaking in its most intimate form.
The marriage bed's a picture relevant
To Christ and church, through calm and storm.
Unfaithfulness destroys more than two lives;
It tears the fabric of community,
Leaves children wounded, wondering why wives
And husbands break their vowed unity.
The Heidelberg would catechize the young:
All unchastity God's curse will bring.
Keep body temple-pure, hold tight your tongue
From lustful speech. Let purity's bell ring.
"You shall not steal" private property
Assumed, not greed but stewardship God gives.
The eighth command protects society
From chaos where the strongest only lives.
But deeper: contentment with our lot,
Trusting Providence for daily bread,
Not grasping, hoarding what we have not got,
But open hand to share what God has spread.
"You shall not bear false witness" truth's foundation
Undergirds all human society.
The ninth command guards reputation,
That precious coin of human dignity.
How quick the tongue to gossip, slander, spin
Half-truths that murder character and name.
The Reformed tradition disciplined within
The church those who brought others into shame.
"You shall not covet" last but far from least,
This tenth word strikes at sin's very root.

Before external sin has been released,
The heart's desire has borne forbidden fruit.
Here, total depravity shows its face:
We cannot keep this law by trying hard.
We need new hearts, created by God's grace,
With new desires by the Spirit charred.
The Ten Words stood like mirror to the soul,
Reflecting back humanity's great need.
Not ladder up to heaven but the toll
That showed the depth of Adam's fatal deed.
The law, Paul said, was tutor unto Christ,
Exposing sin and driving us to flee
To Him whose blood alone has sacrificed
Enough to set law-breakers truly free.
The Reformed tradition held these truths in tension:
The moral law still binds though we are free.
Not for salvation, there was comprehension
That grace alone saves, but sanctity.
The third use of the law: to guide the feet
Of those redeemed, to show them how to live
In gratitude, making their joy complete
As they have freely received and freely give.

CONCLUSION

These poems wound their way through centuries, each thread carefully woven into the grand tapestry of Reformed thought. From Geneva's narrow streets where Calvin's pen scratched late into the night, to Dutch low lands where farmers read their Bibles by candlelight, to Scottish highlands where Presbyterians died rather than bend the knee to earthly kings who claimed dominion over conscience, the truths recovered in the Reformation spread like seed on fertile ground.

These doctrines were not mere abstractions debated in ivory towers. They shaped how ordinary people lived and died. The sovereignty of God transformed how believers faced plague, famine, and war. When the Black Death swept through communities, when children died before their time, when persecution scattered congregations like sheep without shepherds, the Reformed faith offered more than platitudes. It offered a God who worked all things, even the darkest providences, for the good of His people and His own glory.

The Five Solas stood as pillars holding up the whole structure. Scripture alone meant every believer could hold truth in their hands, no longer dependent on a priestly class to interpret God's will. Grace alone stripped away the burden of earning salvation through indulgences, pilgrimages, or perfectionism. Faith alone opened the door to peasant and prince alike. Christ alone removed all other mediators between God and man. To God's glory alone oriented all of life, work, worship, family, art toward its proper end.

Limited atonement, the doctrine that caused such controversy, actually expanded rather than restricted the Gospel's power. Christ's death accomplished what it intended, the certain salvation of His people. Not a general possibility that might fail, but a particular redemption that would not lose a single sheep the Father gave Him. This truth brought comfort to countless souls who wondered if their faith was strong enough, their repentance deep enough, their works good enough. The answer lay not in their grip on Christ but in His grip on them.

The doctrines of grace painted a portrait of salvation that began before time's foundation and stretched into endless eternity. Unconditional election chose a people not for any foreseen merit but from sheer, sovereign love. Total depravity diagnosed the disease that infected every human faculty. Effectual calling broke through spiritual death with resurrection power. Justification declared the guilty righteous based on Another's merit. Adoption brought slaves into the family as beloved children. Sanctification gradually transformed those declared righteous into the image of Christ. Glorification promised that what God began, He would complete.

These truths built communities. In Geneva, in Holland, in Scotland, and in New England, the Reformed faith shaped not just individual hearts but entire societies. The doctrine of vocation meant every legitimate calling served God, the farmer in his field as much as the pastor in his pulpit. The doctrine of common grace meant believers could work alongside unbelievers for the common good. The doctrine of the covenant provided a framework for church membership, baptism, and the raising of children in the faith.

Christian liberty, properly understood, freed believers from man-made traditions while binding them to God's revealed will. The regulative principle kept worship simple and biblical, stripping away the accumulated traditions that obscured the Gospel. The ordinary means of grace, Word, sacrament, and prayer, became the steady diet by which God nourished His people.

The law, no longer a ladder to heaven, became a guide for grateful living. The Ten Commandments showed what love for God and neighbor looked like in concrete terms. The moral law remained binding, not for justification but for direction. Those saved by grace alone still needed to know how to live in ways that pleased their Redeemer.

Church discipline, practiced with tears rather than harshness, sought to restore wandering sheep. Excommunication was medicine, not revenge, designed to bring sinners to repentance and protect the flock from wolves. The marks of a true church is faithful preaching of the Word, right administration of the sacraments, and proper exercise of discipline, which distinguish biblical churches from false ones.

The Reformed tradition never promised ease. It promised truth. It offered a worldview comprehensive enough to address every aspect of life under the sun. From the highest theological speculation to the most mundane daily task, the Reformed faith brought every thought captive to Christ.

This tradition produced preachers like Spurgeon, who filled the Metropolitan Tabernacle with common people hungry for the doctrines of grace. It produced missionaries like David Brainerd, who spent his health bringing the Gospel to Native Americans. It produced theologians like Herman Bavinck, who showed how Reformed thought could engage modern philosophy without compromising biblical truth. It produced pastors like Richard Baxter, who shepherded his flock through civil war and plague with tender, faithful care.

The Reformed faith shaped art and architecture, education and economics, politics and poetry. It inspired Rembrandt's paintings and Bach's fugues. It founded universities and hospitals. It challenged tyrants and comforted sufferers. It built orphanages and freed slaves. Not perfectly, the tradition had its blind spots and sins, but consistently pointing toward a God who ruled all things and called His people to live all of life before His face.

As the centuries passed, the Reformed tradition faced new challenges and opportunities. Liberal theology, biblical criticism, evolutionary theory, two world wars, the sexual revolution, each brought questions the Reformers never faced. Yet the fundamental commitment remained sturdy enough to address new situations. The sovereignty of God, the authority of Scripture, justification by faith alone, the doctrines of grace, these provided a framework robust enough to engage any age.

The tradition continues, not as a museum piece but as a living faith. In churches around the world, in languages the Reformers never heard, believers confess these same truths. They sing Psalms and hymns that echo Reformed convictions. They raise their children on catechisms that distill centuries of biblical reflection. They face their own trials trusting the same sovereign God who upheld their fathers and mothers in the faith.

About the Author

Bruce W. Newcomer is a former Marine and retired pastor at St. Benedict Reformed Church. He has a doctorate in theology and taught Biblical studies and theology before retiring.

www.ingramcontent.com/pod-product-compliance
Lightning Source LLC
Chambersburg PA
CBHW070852050426
42453CB00012B/2160